OVERSEAS MIGRATION

JOHN KOMOLAFE

OVERSEAS

MIGRATION

JOHN KOMOLAFE

Contents

Introduction

Permanent residency is your resident status in a country where you're not a citizen, usually for a permanent period. With permanent residency, you still need immigration control if you don't have a right of abode. A right of abode gives you the power to enter the country without the government's permission and the freedom to live and work there. It is usually given to citizens of a country but sometimes, given to non-citizens who are qualified. With the right of abode, you immediately pass for permanent residency. Having a residency qualifies you for almost the same benefits as the citizens of that country. Not every country issue free residency, but all EU countries have provisions for such provided that person is an EU national who has moved to another EU country and has stayed there for 3 years. The EU has also made provisions for long-term residency rights for non-EU nationals who have legally resided in an EU country for 5 years with a certified means of support, that is, the person is not dependent on that country's social assistance mechanism.

There are various ways you can qualify for permanent residency. Some methods are listed below:

- Owning a business/Investing in one.
- Studying.
- Employment.
- Retirement.
- Asylum.

- Family Reunion.
- Journalists.
- Marriages to citizens.
- Artists, sports figures, and performers.
- PACS (This applies to those who have lived together for more than a year, e.g., married couples).
- Academics.

Marrying a citizen means you'll have a short residency period, and in some instances, none at all before you qualify for citizenship.

Common Requirements for Residency

Most countries in the world have similar criteria in the issuance of residency. Some are:
- Sufficient means
- No criminal records
- Health insurance
- Mustn't be a citizen of that country
- Must be physically present, amongst others.

However, such requirements differ among countries. While some countries like the US has characteristically stringent requirements, others aren't as strong. To qualify for residency in Spain as a non-EU national, after staying there for five years and proving that you have the means to provide for yourself and your family, including health insurance, you will need to provide:
- A valid passport
- Proof of your long-term residence (it could be contract papers

or receipts for rents)

- A certificate of a criminal record that will be issued by the required authority in your home country
- Medical certificate
- Documents related to your marital status (should be translated into Spanish if needed)

With this permit, you have the freedom to work anywhere you like and enjoy all the social services and benefits accruing to citizens of Spain. You can move within other EU member countries for up to 3 months.

In Canada, you'll need a Permanent Residency Card. This card proves your permanent residency status in Canada. To be eligible for the PR Card, you must:

- Permanently stay in Canada for at least 5 years.
- Be present in Canada and not be a citizen of Canada.
- Not be under an active removal order.
- Not be convicted on crimes that are linked to the indiscriminate use of the PR Card.

Each country has rules that suit them. This is what we will treat in this book. This book will furnish you with an overview of different countries and all the information you require for a residency permit.

Andorra

It is called the Principality of Andorra. Majority of the citizens are Christians. Catalan is the country's official language, but it is common to hear Spanish and French spoken on the streets of Andorra la Vella, the country's capital. With a population of about 77,000 people (UN 2019), life expectancy is 81 years for men and 87 for women. Leather constitutes the bulk of exports from this country. Euros is used as their monetary unit, and One Euro equates to a Hundred Cents. Their dialing code is +376 and internet domain is. ad.

A major attraction for foreigners to this country is Andorra's reputable position as a tax haven, one that is comparable to other premier tax havens across the world. It issues Active Residency Permits for those working and Passive Residency Permits for those who are mainly up to date with their financial obligations. It is open to those who're working and those who are retired. Because of the size of Andorra, they grant residency by quota.

Marriage to Andorran nationals may allow you to be a naturalized citizen. However, this is at the government's will after they verify that you have permanently stayed in the Principality for at least 3 years.

Residency Permits

There are 2 main types of permits issued in the Principality. They are active and passive residencies.

Active Residency is issued to people who have come to work in the country on an already existing contract. Passive Residency is granted to retirees or those who want to live in the country without the burden of doing any gainful or professional activity.

The ratio of foreigners to Andorrans in the Principality is high, and because of this, the government devised a means of allowing new residents into the country. They came up with a policy where Residence Permits, known as Residencias, will be issued to applicants, irrespective of whether they are retirees or not, and have an address in the country with a desire to genuinely integrate into being a member of the community. The applicant must have strong financial support or means, such that they don't need payable employment of any form in the country. The Residencia is issued for a one-year period, which is renewable after a year for another 3 years. It is very lengthy process that must be done in the official language of the country. The Immigration Department of the Police handles the applications. Current legislations dictate the process. By default, spending 183 days in the country in a calendar year qualifies you as a resident. It is expected that you apply for Residencia afterward.

A resident in the Principality of Andorra must possess a correct address which shouldn't be a hotel or post box. Your status in the country when you are not a resident is a tourist, and as a tourist, you may own properties and enjoy whatever benefits that come from it for 183 days in a year. Though not enforced in times past, this rule is now being used in checking people in and out of the country.

Procedure for Residence Permit Application

- You must have a residential address in the Principality.
- You must have a bank account that is personally opened by you in the Principality. Third-party arrangements are not allowed.
- Get your form from the Immigration Department of the country's police force. The form must be completed in the official language of the country and attached with the original or notarized copies of the following documents:
  - ✓ Certificate of birth.
  - ✓ Certificate of marriage or divorce.
  - ✓ A certificate that affirms you being of excellent conduct by your home county's police.
  - ✓ Proof of health insurance.
  - ✓ Proof of having an address in Andorra.
  - ✓ Proof of having an income or pension from banks or other relevant institutions.

Processing such applications may take time although there is a receipt that is issued after the documentation process. During this time, you and your fellow applicants should always be in contact with the authorities in Andorra, especially when you are leaving for a trip abroad and when you come back.

The law that governs the issuance of resident permits has, amongst other things, undergone amendments. It is binding on both new citizens and those who have been residing in the county and are not pensioners. They are:

- There is no need for new residents to pay an annual tax.

- Income and assets will not be assessed; neither will there be inheritance tax.

- Heads of households, individuals and other foreign residents will be made to deposit 24,000 Euros with the I.N.A.F, the Andorran agency responsible for finance. You are to make an additional deposit of 6,000 Euros if you are with your spouse. An additional deposit of 6,000 Euros is paid for any other dependents.

Although these deposits don't earn interests, the good news is that these monies will be returned to you when you give up your residence or leave Andorra.

- Those who are applying for the first time must provide evidence of the existence of private healthcare insurance that is at par with the services offered by C.A.S.S, the Certificates of Good Conduct and the Andorran Social Security System. Furthermore, they must show that they possess an annual income that is not less than three times the size of the minimum level of annual salary as pegged by the regulations guiding Andorra's Social Security which is presently at 9,402 Euros each year. Every dependent increases this amount by a factor of one. If you are asked to present a certificate as a means of substantiating the claims you made as you filled in your requirements of having more than 3 times the size of the minimum annual salary, then you must have that same amount in cash in Andorra. Naturally, it'll attract interests at current rates. You may choose to present other acceptable means of proof.

Austria

The Republic of Austria, with its capital at Vienna, is a country of 8.95 million people based on census figures from the United Nations in 2019. Majority of Austrians are Christians, and German is the primary language. The country is stretched over an area of 83,871sq miles, mainly exporting metals, food, paper, livestock, textiles, machinery. Being an EU country, Euro is its currency like Andorra. Life expectancy for men is 79 years for males and 84 years for females. GNI per Capita is pegged at $46,850. The country calling code is +43, and its internet domain is .at.

Unlike other EU countries, the cost of living in Austria is a bit lower. It offers fantastic tax breaks for foreign investors.

Acquiring the citizenship of this country can be done under two main categories:

1. Economic citizenship: You have to show evidence of investing as much as a million dollars into a worthwhile project.

2. Academic citizenship: As an academic, you are offered special concessions and given citizenship on merit.

Residence Permit

They are categorized as

- Antrag sure Erteilung ringer Niederlassungsbweillogung/eines: This is issued to people who have come to Austria for an extended, or permanent stay in Austria. This arises due to employment in Austria, self-employment, you have a family in the country, you are retiring and decide to relocate there, or you are media correspondent and other key personnel.

- Niederlassungsnachweis: This type of residence permit is issued to those who don't have the intention of staying for a long time. It is mostly used by interns, students, artists, short-term employees, etc.

Non-EEA Citizens

For people who aren't members of EEA countries, acquiring the residence permit is compulsory, especially when they intend to stay in the country temporarily. For non-EEA nationals, the condition that predisposes them to be employed is the demand of the Austria job market. These situations are such that foreigners are allowed to work in the absence of any significant public or economic interest that may dictate otherwise. However, there are legislations on the number of foreigners allowed to work in the country. To work here, you need to be employed first. Your employer will proceed to obtain a work permit on your behalf from relevant authorities. When granted, your employer will send it to you. Afterward you will apply for a residence permit.

Austria Visa, Permits, and Immigration

As a European, you are allowed to stay here for as much as you like. EEA nationals don't require a visa to come into the country.

An Entry Visa is given to people who plan to stay in the county temporarily, for not more than six months and have no intention of taking any form of employment in the country. It shouldn't be confused with work authorization. From the first day of January 2006, some exceptions, especially those linked to temporary employment, came into effect.

A resident permit is issued to foreign nationals who plan to stay in the country for more than 6 months. As a student applicant, you need a letter from your school that confirms your status as a student in terms of your behavior and attendance. Transport documents like airline tickets, confirmation of email receipts of your rail or flight are required. When you intend to bring in your vehicle, you will need to present receipts of ferry confirmation, registration documents, and evidence to show you legally own that vehicle, and insurance papers. The embassy may require you to provide an export license.

Immigration Laws for Workers

Changes in the country's politics informed the skepticisms displayed by some companies in the employment of non-EEA nationals. No real changes to the law have been made to this effect. Any applicant who has completed everything required will be approved, regardless of his background. The nature of work documents necessary to process these work permits determines the duration of work permits issued to foreign nationals. The Austrian government requires a lot of papers to process such permits. You need time to gather everything. Documents required must be in German, and where they aren't, they must be translated into the language by certified professionals. In approximately seven weeks, the process will be done. Work permit approvals aren't enough for foreign nationals intending to work in the country. They must apply for residence visas too. Applicants must show that they're qualified for the job they intend to take.

Work permits can be acquired through two ways:

- Secured Work Certificate Application: This is when the applicant works directly under a big company in the country.

- Assignment Permit Application: This type is issued to those who work for companies that provide services to Austrian companies. Whether it is a recruitment company or not is irrelevant. It must provide a service contract as part of the requirements for application. In this case, an accountant of Austrian origin should oversee the applicant's payroll for the payment of all taxes and social security fees.

Australia

The country of 25.2 million people has its capital at Canberra. Sydney is one of its largest cities. The country spreads over an area of 7.7 million sq. Kilometer. English is the country's language, and Christianity is the main religion. United Nations posits that life expectancy in the country is 80 for men and 84 for women. The GNI per Capita of Australia was $43,770 in 2009 (World Bank).

Ores, metals, woods, transport machinery and equipment are some of its major exports. Their international call code is +61. Its internet domain is .au.

Over the years, Australia has developed the habit of treating foreigners with dignity. It has well-thought-out employees sponsored and business migration programs to help those who desire residency and ultimately, citizenship. New Zealanders are given special consideration that bears much resemblance to freedom to move freely in Australia.

Permanent Residency

If you intend to stay permanently in the country, you need to possess a permanent visa. Applying outside the country means you're applying to migrate. Doing it inside the country means you're seeking to be a permanent resident. A permanent resident visa allows you to work. When such is granted to you, your visa label will be attached to your passport to prove your status as a permanent resident of the country.

It is crucial to complete your application with as much information as possible, else, you will prolong the process. The option of lodging online is not available to students who couldn't finish their studies in Australia for reasons ranging from a default from the education provider and those who wish to complete a student visa application with to money at all.

If you are affected by the education provider's default, and you intend to apply online, you have to pay the required fee and meet the various conditions needed for the completion of the online application.

Immigration, Visa, and Work

Strict attention is placed on the volume of people coming into the county. Their qualifications, skills, work experience, and other important variables are constantly monitored.

There are multiple visa options available like the visitors' visa, a long-term visa that allows you work, live, and study in the country, visa based on connections with your family, and regional visa.

Working in Australia isn't tedious. First, you must obtain the right working visa, which could take months to process. However, with an employer, you will get your visa after a few weeks. Specific schemes like the Territory Nominated Visas, STNI visas, and the Australian Business Visas allow you to enter the country as an investor, senior executive or business owner.

An Australian visa is more than a stamp on your passport.

Study

Many courses in this country allow you to obtain work experience and subsequently, a full work permit. A considerable number of people who don't qualify for a work permit or through other immigration routes come to the country as students and never think of going back home. It is a fantastic choice for anyone willing to study overseas.

Belgium

The Kingdom of Belgium is a member of both the EU and EEA. It has a population of 11.5 million people and has the famous city of Brussels as its capital. French, Dutch and German and commonly spoken. It is majorly a Christian country that spreads over an area of 30,528 sq. Kilometer. Men's life expectancy is 78 years, while women is 84. Chemicals, metals, vehicles, diamonds, electrical equipment, and machinery constitute majority of its export. Being a member of the EU, Euros is spent here. In 2009, the World Bank posited that just GNI per Capita was $45,310. Its international dialing code is +32, and its domain is .be.

Requirements for Residency

The Kingdom offers special concessions to investors coming with substantial amounts into the country. In 2000, the period of residency preceding to the attainment of citizenship was reduced to three years, making it one of the shortest in Europe. However, there are different possibilities for the achievement of citizenship by descent.

Residency Visas

There are different types of residency visas or residence permits. It takes a week to process all kinds of residency visas. The following documents will be required:

- A national Paso that is valid for 15 months.

- Two duly completed, dated, and signed visa application forms.
- Two recent passport-sized photographs with your signature behind.
- Two records of your criminal history that covers the last five years and dated within six months.
- A doctor letterheaded medical certificate that is not less than three months old, with the doctor's signature. It should be legalized for $13.

Temporary Residency Visa for Self-Employed or Business Owners

For this visa to be approved, a professional card needs to be accepted. If you intend to start your business in Belgium, you need to apply for a professional card at a Belgium consulate in the area you reside in. It must be obtained before you enter the country. Your residency visa can only be given to you when you present your professional card and other supporting documents.

The following documents must be submitted in person when applying for a professional card:

- A national passport with a validity of 15 months
- Completed, dated, and signed professional card application (three copies)
- Three recently taken passport-size photographs.
- The original copy of your CV and a copy
- An original copy of letters of recommendation and a copy
- An original copy of your University diploma and a copy

- Two original copies of your statewide criminal records issued by the police in the place you reside, spanning five years and less than six months old.
- One original copy of your professional references and an extra copy
- An original copy of a letter that describes what you intend to do in the country and an additional copy. The processes involved in getting this card from the Belgian of the self-employed takes time. It is advised that you tender your request four months before the date you intend to depart.

Students

As a student in the Kingdom, you will require a temporary residency visa. You will have to include in your application, an original and an extra copy of collated and stapled:

- A notarized form of financial support declaration in Dutch/English or French/English singed by your parents or sponsor, guaranteeing payments of your travel, living, medical, educational and other bills.
- If you're a scholar, you must submit proof of scholarship. This should come with your notarized signature.
- A proof from the bank that attests to the solvency of your parents or sponsor, six months payslips, and letter of employment.
- A sum of $6,000 that is constantly available on an annual basis.
- Proof that attests to you being accepted as a regular, research

or full-time student from a fully accredited academic institution.

- If you're a FullBright or BAEF scholar, you will have to attach a letter from your sponsors.

- A written pledge in MS Word or PDF format. You will agree to register with local authorities in the municipality within three days of your arrival in Belgium and leave immediately after your studies. It should come with your notarized signature.

If you're a married student, you will require a package similar to the one above for your spouse and dependents. You will also need an original copy, an extra copy and an extra set of originals of:

- Certificate of marriage with an apostle, birth certificate.

For your children, you'll need:

- Certificate of birth with an apostle.

- Proof of family accommodations acquired before departure.

If either of your spouse or children are not citizens of the US, contact the consulate for further instructions. Students that are in educational institutions not recognized by Belgium and have tendered applications will be referred to the necessary authorities for processing. Restrictions exist, and the time taken to process this will be longer. Ask for your student visa at least three weeks before you depart.

Brazil

The Federative Republic of Brazil is a country of 211 million people (UN, 2019). Portuguese is the official language spoken here, and majority of its people are Christians. With its capital in Brasilia, the country spreads over an area of 8.55 million sq. Kilometers. It is home to big cities like Bahia, Rio de Janeiro amongst others but the biggest is Sao Paulo. In this country, life expectancy for males is 70 and 77 for females. It mainly exports manufactured goods and agricultural produce. Its GNI per Capita in 2009 (World Bank) is $8,040. The Real is the name of the currency here. One real equal a hundred Centavos. +55 is its international dialing code and .br is its internet domain name.

In Brazil, you are qualified for naturalization if:

- You are a citizen of a Portuguese-speaking country.
- You have stayed in the country for a year without a break and have shown high morals.
- You are of any other nationality and have stayed in the county for more than 15 consecutive years with no criminal records.

If you fulfill these conditions, you must meet the following requirements:

- Civil capacity.
- Registration as a permanent resident.
- You are residing in the country for at least four years before your request.
- Be employed or have the means of supporting yourself and

your family.

- Good conduct record.
- No conviction at home and abroad that resulted in a more than one-year sentence.
- Good health.

Reduction of Requirements

If you meet the following conditions, your four-year period might be reduced to one year:

- If you have a Brazilian spouse or child
- If your parents are Brazilians
- If you can provide services needed in Brazil as verified by Justice ministry

Your four-year period might be reduced to two years if you are recommended for professional, artistic, or academic abilities.

- If you own a real estate in the country whose value equals a minimum of 1,000 times the higher reference value, you will get three years reduction.
- If you are a businessman with monies that have the same value to that mentioned above, or have shares of the same worth, in the commercial or civil sector of the economy, specifically earmarked to be used for exploration in industrial or agricultural activities, you will get three years reduction.

Permanent Residence Visa

The following situations may qualify you for a grant of permanent residence.

- Retirement.
- Personal investments.
- Family reunion.
- Transfer of managers or directors.
- Job offer at a Brazilian research, religious or scientific organization.
- You are a manager or director at a religious or social organization.
- You must be in the country within 90 days after you have been given visa.
- Those that hold a permanent visa in Brazil are exempted from the payment of import duties on personal and household goods and professional equipment. This is as long as they arrive the country not earlier than three months and no lesser than six months from the day you came into the country.

All supporting documents that are not from Brazil will be authenticated by the consulate. Supporting documents must be notarized by a Cartorio in Brazil.

Personal Investments

You may end up receiving permanent visas if you meet the following:

1. Invest at least $200,000 in Brazil.

2. Memorandum of association with the company to which the investments will be made.

3. A certificate that shows that you have registered your investment as issued by the country's apex bank.

4. Technical information of the project and plans to absorb Brazilian hands.

Meanwhile, the Ministry of Labor and Employment analysis of the investment projects often focuses on the following aspects:

★ Social interests.

★ Productivity.

★ Nature of investments made and how relevant it is to the transfer of technology.

★ Availability of finances to pursue intended investments.

Retirement

For those wishing to retire in this country, the following conditions must be met:

★ A regular income of at least $2,000 each month, legally transferrable to Brazil. It is on this threshold you will be allowed to have dependents.

★ You will need an extra $1,000 per month if you have more than two dependents.

★ An international passport that is valid for a minimum of six months.

Permanent Work Visa

This is for those involved in religious and social organizations, managers, employees, and academics.

Intra-Company Transfer

A permanent visa is given for work that involves the transfer of directors, managers and executives.

Those working in a Brazilian research, academic or scientific organization with expertise on a particular field are offered permanent visas. This is same for managers and directors of religious and social assistance organizations if they stay away from crime.

Canada

It is common to see a huge number of Christians in its capital, Ottawa. Majority of its 37.4 million (UN, 2019) people are Christians. French is spoken in places like Quebec, and English in Toronto, its largest city. This is so because English and French are its official languages. One Canadian dollar is equals to a hundred cents. This country, spread over an area of 9.9 sq. Kilometers, majorly exports automobile products, forestry products, metals and plastics, agricultural products, energy products amongst others. Life expectancy for men is 79 and 84 for women. Its GNI per Capita in 2009 was $42,170. Its international dialing code is +1 and its internet domain is .ca.

Permanent residency can be obtained in different ways. Some are listed below:

- **Skilled Worker Canadian Immigration**

There are tons of opportunities in this category that will lead to the attainment of permanent residency. You either apply as an individual or through the Provincial Nominee Program. Competition in this category is very strict so be sure you are well qualified before you apply.

- **Canada Business Class Visa**

If you are a business person, you should consider this category.

- **Family Class Canadian Immigration**

To be eligible under this category, you must be sponsored by a citizen of the country or a permanent resident. Your success depends on medical and security checks.

- **Canadian Experience Class Visa**

If you have worked in the country recently or finished from an educational institution in the country, you are likely qualified for this category. This category leads to permanent citizenship. The country wants to hold on to immigrants who have work experience and are conversant with English and French.

This category suits investors and self-employed people who have skills and experiences that will contribute positively to the cultural atmosphere in the country. To qualify as an investor, you must have a CAD$400,000 investment or worth a minimum of CAD$300,000. If you are experienced in farm management, this category is also for you.

- **Provincial Nominee Program Visa**

Skilled workers who intend to migrate to the country must possess the needed skills, experience, and education to hit the ground running and make a quick impact on the country. You must be nominated by a Canadian province or territory to qualify.

Students Visa Requirements

Most students from foreign countries will need a study permit to study in Canada and will have to apply for a temporary residence visa. Exceptions are those who are taking courses that will last less than six months, members of an accredited foreign representative to Canada, and international armed police members. However, every applicant must show:

- ★ Proof of acceptance by an educational institution in Canada.
- ★ Proof of your financial ability to support your stay and transport back to your home country.
- ★ Satisfactory adherence to health requirements.

Student Visa for Short Courses

As stated earlier, you don't need a study visa for courses that are less than six months. But if you intend to stay beyond that time, apply for a study permit before you arrive. You must apply for this if:

- ★ If you are classified as a minor in the province you want to study.
- ★ You plan to work on campus.
- ★ You want to be a part of a co-op or internship scheme.

Study and Work

You won't be needing another work permit if as a foreign national, you intend to combine education and work. Those that possess a valid student visa may work in their campuses, either for a private business or for that institution. Teaching assistants and graduates fall under this category too. They may be allowed to work off-campus without permit under some circumstances.

Dependent Children Studying in Canada

Minor children of foreign nationals who are working or studying in the country will need a study permit for school. The following are exceptions:

* ★ Kids who are going to kindergarten or pre-school.
* ★ Children of those refugees or those claiming to be refugees.
* ★ Children of accredited foreign reps.

Children of primary and secondary school age will require an open study permit while those of university age will need a study permit.

Canadian Business Visa

Immigration applications from foreign nationals who are experienced in business and can make significant contributions to the economy are welcomed. There are three different categories you can apply for as a business person. Each application is relevant to a class and cannot be changed.

* Canadian Business Visa for Investors

Under this category, you must:

- ★ Present evidence of having a minimum of two years of experience in business.
- ★ A net-worth of CAD$1.6m obtained through legal means.
- ★ A refundable investment of C$800,000.
- ★ Proof of the ability to support yourself and your dependents in the country.

Quebec province has its immigration investor scheme.

Business Visa to Canada for Entrepreneurs

This scheme was specifically designed to attract foreign nationals into owning and managing businesses in the country. To qualify, you must prove you have a net worth of C$300,000. You must show that you have operated a qualifying business and superintended a percentage of that company's equity over a stipulated period.

Canadian Visa for Self-employment

To qualify, you need to prove that you have experience in:
- ★ Participating in cultural or athletic activities at a world-class standard.
- ★ Farm management.
- ★ Being self-employed in cultural or athletic activities.
- ★ Journalism, librarianship, performing arts, technical side of broadcasting, and filmmaking.

This country operates a point-based system for selection of potential immigrants. You will need a minimum of 35 points to qualify.

Canada Visitor Visa

To qualify,

- Have a valid passport and be in good health.
- Demonstrate that you wish to stay temporarily.
- Demonstrate your ties with your country of origin. It could be in the form of business, family, or job.
- Proof that you can support yourself as you stay.

If you wish to stay longer than the time you have agreed to, extend your visa 30 days before it expires. It is strictly for recreational purposes.

Entrepreneur Visa

This is the ideal option if you want to set up a business. It offers you a route to permanent residency in the country. It allows you to start to live and work in the country immediately without any job offer. There are no restrictions on the type of work you may seek or do when you arrive. After three years, you may apply for citizenship.

To be eligible,

- You need to show that you have two years of experience in business.
- Show a net worth of a minimum of CD$300,000.
- Commit to own and control at least a third of a pre-defined size business for a minimum of one year.
- Once applied, switching to another route isn't allowed.
- Apply once.

Points System

As stated earlier, the entrepreneur scheme involves a point-based system for skills assessment. Applicants who want to get to Canada through this route are awarded based on their achievements in education, age, experience in business and proficiency in language.

20-35 points are awarded for business experience gained in the five years that precedes the submission of your application.

In education, points are awarded based on your highest academic achievements and the number of years spent in school as outlined in the hierarchy below:

- Maximum marks for Master's/Ph.D. and spending a minimum of 17 years studying full time.
- Two or more Bachelor's degree and at least 15 years in full-time study.
- Apprenticeship, trade certificate, two-year diploma or at least 14 years studying full time.
- One-year bachelors and at least 13 years studying full time.
- A one-year diploma, trade certificate or apprenticeship and at least 13 years studying full time.
- One-year diploma, apprenticeship or trade certificate and at least 12 years studying full time.
- Minimum points for secondary school graduation.

Language Skills

Applying for a work visa requires proficiency in either French or English. If you are proficient in both languages, select one of them as your first language. Points are awarded in the areas of speaking, listening, reading and writing. A maximum of 4 points can be scored for each area for the first elected language and two, for the second.

Age

The highest number of points that can be amassed is limited to a candidate between the ages of 21 and 49. Outside this range, there is a deduction of two points for every year, and no points are awarded to candidates that fall less than 17 and above 53.

Adaptability to Life

You can earn an extra point if you show an uncanny ability to adapt to the life and business in this country. When applying for visa, you can boost your chances by:

- Claiming that you have made an exploratory trip to the country five years before your application.
- Took part in an immigration program that was a joint initiative between federal and provincial authorities.
- In the absence of both, your province will be required to provide documentary evidence.

Dependents

Business visa applications in this country make provisions for the inclusion of the immigration of your spouses and dependents. Dependent children who are unmarried and under the age of 22 may join you in the country. The IIP immigration service provides you with a route to permanent residency. Unlike temporary visas, no kind of work restrictions is placed. No job offer is required. Successful applications will be awarded permanent residency. After three years of immigrating to the country, the immigration service gives you the chance to move from permanent residency and to apply to be a citizen of the country.

China

The People's Republic of China, with its capital in Beijing, is one of the most populated countries in the world with about 1.43 billion people in 2019. Mandarin Chinese is its official language. It is spread over an area of 9.6million sq. kilometers. Buddhism, Christianity, Islam, and Taoism are some of its major religions. China is famous for its export of manufactured goods. To reach it internationally, you will have to dial +86. Yuan, its currency is as famous as the country itself. The internet domain for China is .cn.

Requirements for Visa Eligibility

Visas are divided into business and tourist visas, but various categories exist under each general division.

Business Visa

This gives you a single-entry option, just like the one in the application of a tourist visa, but allows for a multiple entry variant for six months, one year or two years period. To be eligible, you need to have visited the country before. As a first-time applicant, you will be allowed a maximum of a double-entry permit. Applying for the second time may let you receive a six months multiple entry permit. As a third time applicant, you may get a permit for a year. The two-year permit is only available to those who are applying for the 4th time and beyond that.

In this country, visas are designated with letters. Tourist visas are called Chinese L visas and business visas, Chinese F visa. In addition to the already mentioned categories, Chinese immigration authorities issue these types of permits:

- X Visa Category

It is granted to those who wish to study in the country for six months or more. A letter of acceptance from a Chinese educational institution must be provided.

- Z Visa Category

It is also referred to as a Chinese work visa. It is issued to those who intend to stay in the country for an extended period to work. There is a provision for spouse and dependent Immigration through this route. You must add a letter of invitation from your host company or the employing government department.

- D Visa Category

These types are issued to those intending permanent residency. It is applied for within the country and given to those who want to work and live in the country for a long time.

- J Visa Category

They are given to journalists and are split into J1 and J2. The former is for correspondents who have come to stay in the country for a long time and the other for a short period.

- Z Visa Category

It is compulsory for anyone who intends to work in China, irrespective of whether they bring their families or not. It is also issued if you are in commercial entertainment, but in the two cases, it is required that your employer meets the requirements.

First, your employer must submit a certificate to prove you are a foreign expert. Most times, it is as simple as teaching English which needs a certain level of expertise and an accompanying university degree. The company gives you an employment permit and a visa notification letter that you need to provide to the government for processing along with photocopies of your China visa application.

Your family members can also apply and must show a certificate of relationship. The problem with China work visa is that it lasts for 30 days. After this, your employer needs to request for a temporary residence permit which will last for a year.

China immigration visas need a valid passport and documents showing the intention behind your visit. If you intend to stay in the country for a while, you will need to obtain a residence confirmation form which will allow you get temporary housing. You will need an ID card residency form to show that you are a legal immigrant. Interestingly, you, as an investor, may be granted the same visa with say, an asylum seeker.

- China Business Visa

This type is referred to as the category F visa. It is issued to people who are looking to pursue business activities in the country. It covers a lot of events, from business visits to lectures, internships, and scientific research. It is valid for six months. You will require another visa option if you want to stay longer than that time. To apply, you will need a passport that has at least six months validity, photographs and other documents that shows your intention of pursuing business in the country. The more supporting documents you attach, the higher your chances of having your visa approved. Traveling from the US may cost you more, but your multiple-entry options are higher. If you are applying for the first time, you will have to attach your original name passport details on your application.

- X Visa Category

The X visa is for those who want to study in China for half a year or longer. If you come for study for less than six months period, you will require the F visa instead.

To qualify, you will be required to present a passport that has a validity of more than six months, photographs and documents showing that you have been admitted to study in China. You will have to prove you have the right papers to go home, especially if you are not a citizen of your destination country and the needed fees.

Processing usually takes a week for completion. The X visa places restrictions on anyone suffering from a form of mental disorder, AIDS, leprosy, sexually transmitted diseases, and other infections.

- D Visa Category

It is a permanent residence visa that offers the most benefits for a family member. It can be gotten through connections to a Chinese family. It is tough to get without these connections.

- Spouse Visa.

The marriage under question must be registered under Chinese law. Employ the aid of a consultant as it may be confusing without it.

Other categories allow the applicant to bring their family members to the country on the same visa. The country's L visa is sometimes referred to as "family visit visa." It allows visitors to stay with their families in China for a short time.

Dominican Republic

The Dominican Republic is a country spread over an area of 48,072 sq. Kilometers, with a population of 10.73 million people. In Santa Domingo, the capital and in every other city, Spanish and Christianity is majorly spoken and practiced respectively. It is famous for its export of silver, coffee, sugar, gold, tobacco, ferronickel amongst others. Life expectancy for males is 70 and 76 for female. Its GNI per Capita in 2009 was $4,510. Its internet domain is .do, and international dialing code is +1809.

It is an economic member of OECS, Organization of Eastern Caribbean States. Here, acquiring residency is easy. Being a citizen of one of the OECS member states will allow you to work and live in all nine member states except for British Virgin Islands and Anguilla. To qualify for economic citizenship, you will be required to pay a fee between $100,000 and $150,000 depending on whether you are single or have a family. It takes two to three months.

Economic Citizenship/Family Option

Under this, the investor pays $150,000, qualifying the investor, his spouse, and two children under the age of 18 for economic citizenship. An addition of $25,000 is required for children above 18 but below 25. Another $25,000 cash contributions will be required for any other child below 25. 30% of the investment ($50,000) will be designated for private sector projects that are government approved and the remaining 60% ($100,000) for projects in the public sector. Any additional payments made over the $150,000 will be earmarked for government financing.

Economic Citizenship/ Single Option

The investor under this option is the sole applicant for the citizenship irrespective of his marital status. A single investor will be required to invest $100,000. Half will be moved to projects in the public sector and the other half towards private sector projects approved by the government.

Requirements

1. Investors must be under 25 and possess outstanding character.
2. You must provide all necessary documents.
3. An application letter for economic citizenship addressed to the Ministry of Legal Affairs, Labor and Immigration stating why you want to invest.
4. The investor or the parents/guardians of kids below 18 must sign all forms
5. Basic knowledge of English
6. Deposit into the right account at the National Commercial Bank of Dominica the amount you want to invest.
7. Supporting documents must be in English, and a public notary must certify photocopies.
8. The lodged amount be withdrawn unless the application was rejected, withdrawn or approved.

9. If it is withdrawn or rejected, the application will be refunded. If the rejection was because of false information, the investment shall be forfeited.

10. If it is refused, every sum except fees paid for application of economic citizenship will be paid back within one month.

11. A letter requesting a refund will be addressed to the finance minister.

12. The process may take eight weeks.

13. All investors must have a promoter or agent. Overseas sponsors must work with local ones.

United Arab Emirates

Permanent residency can be obtained by employment, business activities and family connections. Immigration laws in this country vary based on the nature of the visa appointment and the applicant's country of origin.

- Work Visa

It is an employer-led process. It is of different types and durations and the kind of job they allow.

- Student Visa

It allows you to live and study in the country. To qualify, you must be enrolled in a sponsoring educational center.

- Family Visa

There are different types of visa that are designed for married people and other members of the family. It usually involves some form of sponsorship from a family member that is already residing in the country.

- Business Visa

There are different categories for businessmen and investors making considerable investments in the country. It lasts for a maximum of 3 years. It includes visas for long-term and short term for business trips. It is granted provided the applicant provides proof of business practices or investments.

Examples of such categories are investor visa that is granted to those willing to make investments and business partner visa for those involved in business activities. The difference between both visas is that the partner visa requires you to own a certain number of shares in a company. Security deposit payments are needed too.

- Visas for employment

It is your best path to immigration. An initial application gives you a three-year visa which can be extended indefinitely.

Types of Dubai Work Visa

The main category of the Dubai work visa is the Residence Permits for employment issued by an employer." It allows an employee to work in the private sector for up to three years. As with every process, you need to provide a wide range of documents to support your application.

There are permits designed for workers in the public sector too. It lasts for three years, like the public sector. Documents required in this category differ significantly from others. However, this category is easy to obtain.

The second category is the short-term visa. It allows you to work in the country for a short-term but gives you the freedom to live and work in the country.

Other types of business visas into the country caters for some specific needs. Mission Visa is a short-term visa available for businesspeople and professionals. If you have a business relationship with a company based in the country, you may be qualified for a multiple entry visa. It allows you to enter and leave the country as many times as possible.

- Student Visa

Students attending a school in the country may be allowed to apply for a visa based on different reasons. It could be a family-sponsored visa or an educational institution sponsored visa. They are both available to full-time students. There are provisions for those coming to study in the country for a short time.

- Spouse/Child Visa

It is referred to as "Residence Permits for expatriate families in the UAE." Under this, a spouse or a child can stay for up to three years. Evidence of the sponsor's residence is essential.

- Family Visa

It is designed for parents and second-degree relatives. Under this kind of visa, a resident of the country is allowed to sponsor family members to live in the country for one year at most. Security deposits and other supporting documents are required.

Other types of short-term visas for family members exist. It js indicated with the letter From and requires the sponsorship of a resident family member. A deposit, refundable upon the visitor's departure, is usually needed.

France

According to the UN, the population of the French Republic is about 65.2million in 2019. Its capital, Paris, is famous for being a love paradise. French and Christianity is majorly spoken and practiced respectively. Stretched over an area of 543, 965 sq. Kilometers, the country mainly exports agricultural products, transport equipment amongst others. As a member of the European Union, Euro is its currency. Life expectancy is 79 years for men and 85 for women. In 2009, World Bank stated its GNI per Capita to be $42,680. Its international dialing code is +33 and its domain name is .fr.

There are different types of residency permits in this country and each one confers on you a defined status during your stay in the country. You need to know which one you need and apply for it accordingly.

- Temporary Residency Permits

A Carte de sejour tomporaire allows you stay for a maximum period of one year. There are different types of temporary residency permits with several status that includes:

- A one-year visa for your spouse and minor child, if you have been working in the country for 18 months. It is a visitor's visa and it isn't enough a permission to work. You must prove your ability to support yourself during your stay.

- Students from non-EU and EEA countries require student visa. You can apply for this at the nearest French consulate. You need to be sufficiently supported financially during your stay. You are allowed to work as you study. For international students coming from non-EEA and EU countries, and are not Swiss nationals, they have the option of accepting paid jobs for up to 60% of the work year.

- Employee: You will need a work permit to get this one.

- Self-employed: This type gives you the freedom to do your professional activities. You need to be authorized to practice such activities. It is especially difficult for non-EEA/EU and Swiss nationals. You have to contact the French consulate close to you for more information.

- Trader: Gives you the chance to trade and do other commercial activities. You need to have received the requisite authorisation before you are granted this visa.

- Scientific: This type of visa gives you the chance to enter the country regularly and live in it for scientific research or to teach at university level. You will need to present a certificate issued to you by a research institute or university, stating your qualifications and the duration you intend to stay.

- Private or family purposes: You may receive this type if:

- You're a minor permanent residency holder,

- A spouse to a holder and you legally entered France.

- You are a minor living in France 15.

- The spouse of a French national and you entered legally.

- One of the parents of a child who is a French national and the child depends on you.

A permanent residency allows you to live in France permanently. It is valid for up to 10 years and is renewable. An EU national who has lived in the country for 5 or more years is entitled to permanent residency and won't be required to provide proof of their income or employment. A time may come where you will be needed to provide such proofs to keep your residency. You can also obtain permanent residency through marriage to a French national.

Germany

The Federal Republic of Germany is a country located in the central and western part of Europe. With its capital and its largest city in Berlin, the country is home to about 83.5 million people (2019 UN estimate). German is its main language and Christianity is its main religion. Spread over an area of 357,386 square kilometers, the country is famous for its export of vehicles, machinery, rubber and plastics, economic products and electrical equipment. Life expectancy in 2016 was 79 for males and 83 for females according to the WHO.

$51,760 was its GNI per Capita in 2017. It spends Euros, uses +49 dialing code and .de is its internet domain.

Residency Requirements

Immigration laws in this country are complex and sometimes confusing. It requires a lot of documentation so you'll do well to start preparing before you move to Germany.

EU nationals and other nationals don't require visas before coming into Germany. The kind of visa you get will affect your residency rights, so choose well.

If you plan to work and live in the country, you will have to register at a local residence registration office. Everyone staying in Germany, excluding EU nationals and citizens of Norway, Iceland, Switzerland and Liechtenstein, for more than 3 months must get a residence permit. When applying for a permit, you will be required to provide:

- A valid ID or passport with visa.

- Two biometric passport photographs.

- Your birth and marriage certificate, as applicable.

- Health insurance proof.

- Registration of residence.

- Proof that you can support yourself. It is usually a letter from your employer and in the case of those who are not employed and are students, a proof of adequate financial resources is required, usually around €700/month.

- A certificate of good conduct from your home country.

- Health certificate for residence permit.

You will have to prove your status during your stay in the country by providing the following documents:

- Employees: Proof of employment like an employment contract.

- Students: Proof of registration at a university.

- Self-employed: Like a Membership of a trade body.

- Frontier workers: They are those working in Germany who live in another country that is an EU member and go back there at least once during the week. As a frontier worker, you will need to provide proof of your employment and proof that you reside in that country.

Before going to apply at your local Immigration office, be sure to check out details because requirements change. There is an interview that lasts around 10 minutes if everything goes well. It takes a week or two at most to process. Your residence permit is only valid when it is displayed with your national identity documents. You can take up employment if your residence permits expressly allows you to do so.

The Residence Act differentiates between three residence titles:

- Unlimited settlement permit: This type of permit is most times the basis of some people's stay in the country because after holding this title for a while and meeting some conditions, they can apply for unlimited permit. It is issued for specific reasons.

- Limited settlement permit with a special title via the EU Blue Card: The Blue Card is a special title that allows you, from a third-world country, to stay in Germany for four years. To get this, you'll need a university degree or something similar.

- Permanent stay permit for EU: There are no restrictions. You can take up gainful employment. You apply as soon as you meet all conditions like:

  - Having a residence permit for at least 5 years.

  - Being employed for five years with payments of social contributions.

  - Secure means of living.

  - Secure accommodations for you and your family.

  - Adequate knowledge of German.

  - Sufficient knowledge of Germany's social and legal system.

For spouses, it is enough that their partners are employed and pays contributions for social insurance but children are generally entitled to a permit of this kind if at aged 16, they had a residence permit for five years.

Study

Foreign nationals can be issued a residence permit for study. It may be for 3 months and this can be extended at the discretion of German authorities. Those who are in universities can obtain a permit of two years extendable to the end of their studies. Students can work for 120 days or 240 half days during this time. Visa can be extended for 18 months to allow students seek employment after studies.

Residence permits can be issued to those seeking vocational training. It depends on approval from the Federal Employment Agency. On completion, visa can be extended for 18 months for the purpose of seeking employment depending on the qualifications.

Malta

The Republic of Malta is a majorly Catholic country with a population of about 440,000 people in 2019 (UN estimate). Its capital is Valletta. It is a relatively small country that covers an area of 316sq. Kilometers. To reach the country internationally, +356 is the number to dial. Being a European country, Euros is accepted as a means of exchange. The country has the distinction of being the 10th smallest country in the world. The country is a popular tourist destination with three UNESCO heritage sites. Data gotten from the World Health Organization showed that life expectancy in the country is 80 for males and 83 for females. The country's domain name is .mt.

Malta is famous for being the base for the itinerant order of the crusader knights. It is home to several beautiful beaches. Its soothing weather makes it a top holiday destination. From enjoying the rigours that come with fishing in Marsaxlokk to the romantic scenery at Mellieha and the beautiful beaches and ancient temples in Valletta to maritime museums, Malta is the place you want to be, for study, work or business.

It is vital to understand the legal requirements before going to Malta. The nature of your journey and your nationality will define the type of visa or permit you will pursue. Below are some requirements you have to meet.

Visa Requirements

- You must have the requisite means of supporting yourself economically

- The data you submitted during the application process must be correct

- You must provide the information that states your reason for visiting or coming to stay in the country. You may be denied entry on matters related to national security or public policy.

- Citizens of the following countries won't need a visa to enter Malta provided their stay is for about three months. They are: EU national or a national of Lithuania, Israel, Japan, Brazil,

Andora, Brunei, Bolivia, El Salvador, Malaysia, Chile, Canada, New Zealand, Monaco, Croatia, San Marino, United States of America, Republic of Korea, Norway, Guatemala, Uruguay, Vatican City, Liechtenstein, Iceland, Argentina, Australia, Venezuela, Honduras, Panama, Paraguay, Switzerland, Mexico, Nicaragua, and Singapore. Note that Chinese who hold the Hong Kong Special Administrative Region Identification do not require visas.

If you are not from one of the countries above, you will need a visa to enter the country. A standard list of countries for which visa is a requirement is in the country's Ministry of Foreign Affairs website.

How to Apply for Malta Visa

Before you embark on your journey to Malta, you have to apply for a visa at the Maltese embassy in your country of residence. You can also apply at an embassy of an EU member state where Malta has a representation agreement. It is advised that you tender your application early because the process can take 15 days or more to process. If there is no Maltese embassy in the country you reside in, you can apply directly to the country's Foreign Affairs Ministry. There is a downloadable visa application form on their website. After filling it with the needed information, you can send this form to the police commissioner alongside a photocopy of your passport and other required documents.

You will receive a faxed statement from the immigration police, telling you if your application has been approved or not. If your application were approved, you would show the airline the letter before you travel. Your visa will be given to you when you arrive.

Visa Types

If you are going to Malta for leisure, you might be required to come with a travel visa. There are three types of travel visa available:

- Schengen Visas: This type of visa is valid in all member states who are signatories to the Schengen treaty. These visas may be airport transit visas, transit visas that are valid for 24 hours only, and short-stay visas that are valid for up to 90 days with allowances for single and multiple entries.

- Limited Territorial Validity Visas (LTV): This type of visa is valid only in Schengen state where the visa was issued. Sometimes, it is for specific cases of emergency, and it is hard to apply for.

- Long Stay or national visas: This type of visa is issued for visits that will exceed 90 days. It allows you to travel freely in other Schengen countries, but only for five days.

If you are from a non-EU country and wish to stay in the country for more than 90 days, you will be given a "national" visa before you are given a residence permit.

You will be required to present the following documents for your visa application:

- A visa application form which you must complete in a

triplicated form.

- A valid passport.

- A re-entry visa to the country you will like to travel to that is valid.

- A return ticket confirmation.

- Two recently taken and identical passport photographs.

Work Visas and Permits

Now known as "employment licenses," it is issued by the Employment and Training Corporation. You have to acquire it before you are allowed to work in the country legally. It is distinctive because the employer makes the application, not the job seeker. They are necessary for any non-EU foreigner desirous of working in the country. If you are caught without it, your employers will be penalized and be made to pay a hefty fine, and you will be deported.

For EU citizens, except for Croatia, European Economic Area member states, and Swiss Citizens, there is no requirement for them to obtain employment licenses before they are allowed to work in the country. However, it is recommended that they contact EURES advisors via their portal to know the requirements they must meet before they are allowed to work in the country.

If you have been granted residency in the country, and you are not an EU, EEA or Swiss national, you have to register as a job-seeker. You must complete a registration form called ETC35. However, completion of this form does not guarantee that you will be hired or be granted an employment license. Note that the country has a job pool that is restricted for workers who are Third Country Nationals (TCN). It holds that for some jobs in some areas (as hosted here), offers must first be open to Nationals of the country and citizens of the EU. When the search to get a qualified candidate for the position advertised in the right forums and for the adequate amount of time fails, the search will be extended to include foreign nationals. They will be required to apply for employment licenses on behalf of successful candidates.

After filling form ETC35, you are to take it to this address: "Valletta Access, Victoria Job Center, Gozo." There you will be asked to provide documents that include ID card, the form itself, your curriculum vitae or resume, and any certification you possess.

How to apply for an employment license

If you are a third-country national, your employer will be required to fill out and submit an application form via mail or physical submission to the unit in charge of employment license. The following documents are required:

- Application form.

- Curriculum Vitae.

- References.

- Description of position.

- One passport photograph.

- One copy of a valid visa.

- A copy of your travel document.

- A copy of your certificates, letters of recommendation, etc.

- A cover letter by your employer that shows the site you will be working at/from.

- Paid fee.

- A detailed vacancy report that serves as evidence showing that EEA/Maltese or Swiss nationals were sought to fill that position.

You may be required to provide other documents. You can read the various guidelines guiding the application and issuance of an employment license on the government website.

If your application is rejected, a letter will be posted to you within 15 days of your application. If it's approved, it will be sent to the concerned authorities who normally take between four to six weeks to process it. As soon as you are issued, you will be informed, and an engagement form generated showing the first day your license is valid.

Employment licenses are non-transferable. It means that an employer cannot transfer one license to a different worker if that worker quits the job permanently. These licenses are valid for one year and can be renewed via an application, an evidence of insurance, and tax payments. The application must be made eight weeks before the expiry of the present license. If the application is sent later than this time and the current license expires, you cannot work until you renew your license.

Student Visa

Every student going to study in or visit Malta requires a visa. However, some nationalities require visas only when their stay will last for more than three months. Students who are EU nationals can apply for a student visa through a process that is identical to that of the work or travel visa. Visas are not needed if you are staying for less than three months.

On the other hand, non-EU students need to apply for a visa regardless of the length of time they are staying for. It is advised that as a non-EU student, you apply for a Schengen visa as this will allow you to travel to other member states.

You must complement your visa application process with the necessary documentation. It will boost your chances of acceptance as the embassy doesn't consider half of the application it gets. The following is a list of document you will be required to provide:

- ✓ An application form completed by you.

- ✓ A passport/travel document that is valid.

- ✓ Identical coloured passport photographs that should be less than six months and adheres to the requirements of the embassy (2 copies).

✓ A letter from your university faculty that proves your status as a student.

✓ Evidence of travel insurance throughout your stay. The insurance company will give you a certificate you will use in your application.

✓ Proof of your travel plans. The country's embassy insists that you must have booked your travel (air, rail, ferry, etc) before you make any applications for visa.

✓ Proof of accommodation.

✓ Proof that you have the requisite financial means to support your stay. The law states that you have a daily sum of at least €30. You will need to present your bank statements, traveller's cheque, wage slips for the last three months and other corresponding documents to prove your financial capacity.

✓ An application fee for your Schengen visa.

✓ A special delivery envelope addressed to yourself so that the embassy can post back your document once a decision has been reached.

✓ Photocopies of all the documents you have provided. You will need to provide originals and photocopies.

Residency

In Malta, there are two available options for residency. The first is the ordinary residency. This type is for people who are already living in the country, applying for a job permit and seeking a job. It is also available for those who want to take advantage of the country's low tax jurisdiction and register it as their tax residence. Here, as a work permit is granted, you are granted residence automatically, and it covers your spouse. However, it doesn't mean your spouse is qualified for a work permit.

The second is called "permanent residency." It allows you to stay in the country for as long as you like but isn't enough legal reason to allow you to work. A physical residence is not required from you, and you can come and go as much as you like. There are financial, and property conditions that you must meet that include having a net worth of 349,000 Euros or 23,000 as annual income, a report showing your good character, and an interview process. Permanent residents are required to open and operate an account in which they must make a yearly minimum deposit which is income taxed. Deposits over this minimum will not be taxed.

United Kingdom (EU) (EEA)

The United Kingdom is a combination of England, Scotland, Wales, and Northern Ireland. 2019 estimate of its population is about 67.6

million by the UN. It is home to many famous cities like Liverpool, Newcastle amongst others, with London as its capital. English is the predominant language, and Christianity is the dominant religion practiced. As one of the world's largest economies, the country is famous for its exports of financial services, maritime services, agricultural products, vehicles, aircraft, mechanical equipment, medical equipment amongst others. Sitting on an area of 543,965 sq kilometers, the World Bank reported its GNI per Capita as $44,930 in 2018. Current life expectancy is 79 years for men and 82 years for women. The Pound Sterling is the currency used in this country, and its international dialing code is +44. Its internet domain is .uk.

If you are not a professional, it might be challenging to obtain a UK visa. The visa program is separated into tiers. They are:

- Tier 1 for the highly skilled/enterpreneurs
- Tier 2 for sponsored workers
- Tier 4 for student's visa
- Tier 5 for temporary workers

Work visas are part of the UK's point-based system, and most times, they provide an opportunity for visa extension and may ultimately culminate in permanent residency.

Tier 1 (Enterpreneur Visa)

This visa is for successful enterpreneurs who wish to carry out their trade in the UK. In this Tier, there are provisions for people who want to come for a short business trip in "Business Visitors Visa" and high net-worth individuals interested in making significant financial investment in the country in "investor visa." With Tier 1 visa, highly skilled workers in the country have the chance to prolong their stay.

Tier 2

This visa allows highly skilled workers with a job offer in the UK to migrate to the country. After living and working in the country for five years under a Tier 2 visa, you may qualify for Indefinite Leave to Remain (ILR). After another year, you may be eligible for naturalization as a citizen. As an employee, you will be sponsored by your employer. Before you can obtain this visa as a non-EEA national, you must have a job offer, and your employer has to present a Certificate of Sponsorship obtained from the authorities. The responsibility of making sure that you are eligible for the position and your accountability for infractions rests on your employer.

Under the "Intra company transfer" feature, the Tier 2 visa allows the transfer of individuals from an overseas branch of a UK company into the country.

The Minister of Religion Tier 2 Visa allows those that work in the religious industry with a pending job offer from an organization in the UK to live and work in the country as sponsored workers.

The Tier 2 sportsperson visa allows coaches and athletes with international exposure and success to live and work in the country as sponsored workers.

Tier 4 (Students Visa)

This visa is for those who are above 16 years and want to study in the UK. It is a point-based scheme that allows:

- Students over the age of 16 to study in an educational institution in the country under the "Adult Student Visa."
- Students below the age of 16 to do a full-time study in the country under an educational provider under the "Child Student Visa."

The course you are applying to study must be the one that leads to an accredited qualification at the appropriate level. It must be full-time too. The following is a list of the acceptable level of courses:

- Level 3 or higher in the National Qualifications Framework in England, Wales and Northern Ireland. If your course provider is not a highly classed sponsor, then your course would need to be at Level 4 NQF at least.
- Level 6 or higher in the Scottish Credit and Qualifications Framework (SCQF).
- A course in English Language at any level where a student is under government sponsorship.
- Courses that have work placements. These work placements should not exceed more than 50% of the course and are assessed as part of the course.
- A course in English Language at level B2 or above in the Common European Framework of Reference for Languages.

As a student who is more than 18 years old, you can't spend more than three years in the UK for your bachelor's degree. However, there are exceptions.

When your application is successful, you will be given leave to stay in the UK for the time you are studying plus extra time, as the type and length of your course demands. If your course is going to last for six months or longer than that, you can arrive the country up to a month before the commencement of your course. If not, you will only come seven days before it starts. That is the general rule.

Conditions that must be fulfilled before you stay in the UK include:

- No recourse to public fund.
- Registration with police.
- No study apart from your course.
- Employment is allowed in a few circumstances.

Generally, the Tier 4 visa doesn't lead to a settlement. If you have stayed in the country for more than ten years legally, you may qualify for settlement.

Tier 5 (Temporary Worker)

This visa category covers people coming to do sports or entertain people for not more than 12 months, those doing voluntary work for not more than 6 months, those doing religious work, those coming to provide services allowed by international law and those coming to the country through schemes authorised by the government that aims at sharing knowledge and experience. All applicants under this visa category require a UK based sponsor that wishes to employ them.

- Attributes

Applicants must score 30 points for attributes. It is awarded based on the applicant holding a valid Tier 5 Certificate of Sponsorship.

- Attributes for Tier 5 (Creative and Sporting)

This category is for professionals in the sporting and creative sector who have come to stay in the country for a short time. As a sportsperson, you must be internationally established and have competed at the highest level, or your employment would contribute to the development of your sport in the United Kingdom. If you are a coach, you must have the qualifications to fill the role. You can come with your entourage using a group certificate of sponsorship. Your entourage may include those whose work is directly related to yours and have the requisite technical skills.

- Tier 5 (Charity Worker)

This is issued to applicants who have pledged to undertake an unpaid job in line with the aims of a sponsor in the United Kingdom. Emphasis is on the applicants coming to do voluntary work and not paid work of any kind.

- Tier 5 (Religious Workers)

This is for those coming to work temporarily in the religious sector. Before you are issued a Certificate of Sponsorship, your sponsor will have to guarantee that you:

- ✓ Are qualified to do the job.
- ✓ Will work only in the specified location except when you are working in supplementary employment provision.
- ✓ Will comply with the conditions that allow for your stay in the country and will leave it as soon as it appears.
- ✓ Will not be displacing or denying employment to any qualified member of the labour force.
- ✓ Accept the sponsor's responsibilities on you.
- ✓ Only intend to take up employment as a religious worker.

- Tier 5 (Government Authorised Exchange)

This is issued to those coming to the United Kingdom through legal schemes that aim to share knowledge, experiences through work placements while, at the same time, exploring the social and cultural background and settings of the United Kingdom. It is not a chance at employment and not a way to bring unskilled labour to the UK. Individual employers and organizations are not allowed to bring individuals even if they are licensed as sponsors under any tier.

- Tier 5 (International Agreement)

This is issued to applicants coming to the UK to provide services allowed under international law. Examples are employees of overseas government and international organization, member of staff of a diplomatic mission with defined diplomatic privileges and immunity, an employee of an international organization working in the United Kingdom with certain rights as recognized by the law, intending to work full-time, without taking up any other employment and will leave the country as soon as the permission to stay in the country expires.

All applicants to Tier 5 must be able to take care of themselves and their dependents financially. It is an essential requirement for your application to be successful. Even if you attained the mandatory 30 points for your certificate of sponsorship, your application will be refused if you don't get the ten required points allocated to the fulfillment of this condition.

If your application is refused outside the United Kingdom, it doesn't guarantee you an immediate appeal. However, you can file an appeal on one or more of the following grounds as outlined in Section

84(1)(b) and (c) of the Nationality, Immigration and Asylum Act of 2002 that the decision to deny you entry was unlawful per the provisions of Section 19B of the Race Relations Act 1976(c.74) and/or Section 6 of the Human rights act of 1998.

EEA Family Permit

All nationals of EEA countries and Swiss citizens are free to come into the country without visas. Non-EEA relatives of EEA nationals working and living in the UK need to apply for and be granted an EEA family permit before they will be allowed to stay with their families in the UK.

Residence Permits for EEA and Swiss nationals

EU laws allow a national of an EEA country and Switzerland to live and work in the country. There is a need for the presentation of passport or national identity card. You have the right to, amongst other things, accept work, be self-employed, set up your business, manage your company, support yourself with public funds, etc. For your EEA family members, you will need to apply for a residence document called ETC1 that is valid for 5 years. However, it can be issued for shorter periods. Your non-EEA family members need to apply for an EEA family permit before they are allowed to travel to the UK if they are coming to stay with you for a long time or permanently. Without this permit, they may be refused entry into the country. You must apply for the permit in a British embassy in the country your non-EEA family member resides. They don't need to register with the police on arrival neither do they need a work permit. There are documents you need to submit for a family permit like your passport or national identity card, residence permit, your family members passports, proofs of your relationship with your family member and a host of others.

There are other types of visas that includes the partner visa, visitor visa, tourist visa, family visitor visa, business visitor visa, marriage visitor visa, student visitor visa, child visitor visa, medical visitor visa, sports visitor visa, entertainer visitor visa, parents of a child at school visa, ancestry visa, and many more. Some requirements must be met for each type of visa. The nature of your visit to the kingdom goes a long way in defining the type of visa you will apply for.

Overstayers

An overstayer is one that was granted limited leave to stay in the country but didn't leave when the date expired or asked for an extension. It is an offence as captured in s.24(1)(b)(I) of the Immigration Act or 1971, Section 24(1A) of the 1971 Act as inserted by s.6(1) of the Immigration Act of 1988. Overstayers in the UK are of different types viz those that have the intention of overstaying the time they entered the country, those that overstayed due to an error in judgment (time, date), and those that were prevented from staying within the requisite timeframe due to circumstances beyond control. Anyone in any of the above situations is called an "illegal entrant" and if apprehended by UK law enforcement agencies, will be made to face the law. He will be ejected from the country and in some cases, prison time or fine comes before.

Retirement

If you are retired person, aged 60 or above, with the required financial capacity, you may come and live in the UK. You must possess an investment or rental income that is worth more than Twenty-five Thousand Pounds per year. You must provide proofs that show close relationship between you and the UK. It could be your relatives in the country, business connections, previous residence or a strong sense of attachment to the identity of the United Kingdom. As an EEA or Swiss national, you will be granted an unconditional right to reside in the country. The law that guides this part states that you will be required to stop all work commitments in the UK and abroad. However, there are options for you if you want to venture into business.

Asylum

All applications are in accordance to the 1951 UN convention that defines a refugee as "a person who owing to a well-founded fear of being persecuted for reasons of race, religion, nationality, membership of a particular social group or political opinion, is outside the country of his nationality, and is unable or, owing to such fear, is unwilling to avail himself of the protection of that country. Application registration cards (ARC's) are issued to asylum seekers as a means to boost identification and reduce cases of forgery. The main features of asylum in the UK include, amongst other things,

- Fair hearings for all claims
- Claimants must be in touch with regular authorities

- Claimants may be detained for all or part of the time.
- Claimants may leave the country if their application was rejected.

United States of America

The United States of America is famed as one of the world's most influential country. Its motto, "In God we trust," gives credence to the fact that it is a Christian majority country. Its population is also on the high side with the United Nations in 2019 stating a population of 329 million. From its capital in Washington DC, and other states, machinery, equipment, agricultural products, coins, metal, medical technology, vehicle, oil, aircraft, spacecraft, pharmaceuticals, organic chemicals amongst others are exported. The size of the US is 543,965sq kilometers. The country is home to many famous cities like California, New York, Texas and of course, English is the official language. Life expectancy is 79 for men and 85 for women according to the United Nations. Data from World Bank showed it's GNI per Capita in 2018 to be $63,390. Its internet domain is .us and its international dialing code is +1.

If you intend to enter the country as a tourist or for a quick business and your country isn't a participant in the US visa waiver program, you will have to apply for a B-1 business visa or a B-2 tourist visa. On the other hand, if you intend to work and live in the country for a long time, your employer will have to file a US work petition visa on your behalf. Examples are:

- H-1B visa for many professional occupations
- TN Visa for professionals of Canadian and Mexican descent
- E-3 visa for professionals of Australian origin
- R-1 visas for religious workers
- I visa for journalists amongst others.

If you intend to invest in a US-based business, E-1 and E-2 visas are options you can choose from. They have a 5 years validity and can be renewed indefinitely throughout the business' time of operations. Study visa allows academic students to live in the country. Non-academic/vocational students have F-1 and M-1 visas that enable them to study in the country.

J-1 visa is most times an excellent option for postgraduate training and work experience. There are other special visas for people like athletes, diplomats, and government officials, members of an entertainment group, individuals with extraordinary abilities in the field of science, arts, education, and business.

For those who want to migrate permanently to the US, there are several available options to gain lawful entry into the country permanently, commonly referred to as "Green Card". The paths include family ties, investment, employment and an annual lottery called the Diversity Visa Lottery.

Green Card

The Diversity Immigration Visa Program, also known as the Green Card Lottery, has a pool of 55,000 available visas yearly for people who are randomly selected and those who meet the requirements of countries with low rates of Immigration to the US. It is conducted by the US State Department and runs from October to the beginning of November. Laws in the US allows permanent residents and citizens to petition for some residents to live in the country permanently, allowing them to obtain a Green Card without necessarily returning home. You can get a Green Card through your family members by:

1. Being an immediate relative of a citizen of the United States of America.
2. Being a family member of a citizen of the United States in a category of preference.
3. Being a family member of a US citizen in a special category.

You can also obtain your Green Card through work. Your employer will have to certify that the job you are taking cannot be done by a local worker. But workers with high skills and technical abilities are sometimes given preferential treatments and may be allowed to self-petition for permanent residency. Special jobs that will get you the Green Card includes Afghan/Iraqi translators, Religious Workers, Panama Canal employees, and NATO-6 non-immigrants. Foreign investors may get Green Cards if their business is set up to create new jobs.

Work Visas

For employment-based immigration, there are a number of visa options available. Some are:

- EB-1 visas for persons with extraordinary abilities,

outstanding professors and researchers.

- EB-2 and EB-3 visas: Workers with advanced degrees are eligible for EB-2 visas while those with bachelor's and two years' work experience qualify for EB-3. Those with lesser qualifications fall into the "Other Workers" category.

The processes involved in the application for permanent residency under this category is often long and tedious. This explains why some workers enter the country with non-immigrant visa like H-1B visa and later, start the process for permanent residency.

- EB-4 visas for religious workers and other special Immigrants.

- EB-5 visas is for foreign entrepreneurs who will invest a million dollars in the US that will create 10 new jobs for workers in the United States within two years of its establishment.

Application to live permanently and work in the US is a tedious process. It sometimes involves about three different applications with three different government agencies over a period that takes years.

Citizenship

Through naturalization, people who have lived permanently in the US for five years or three for those whose spouses are US citizens, can become citizens of the country. They must prove that they have a basic understanding of the history and government of the United States of America and must have a basic understanding of English. Below is a brief guide on the US Citizenship and Immigration Services (USCIS), the government agency charged with the responsibility of attending to all immigration issues.

The services are divided into three categories viz, Visa, Green Cards and Citizenship.

- Visa: It is called "non-immigrant visa" to differentiate them from Green Cards. While Green Card permanent, visa is temporary.

- Citizenship: To qualify, you must have been living in the country for a long time, from three to five years.

Citizenship and Immigration Services

- Immigration: Regardless of whether they want to work or not, those who want to permanently immigrate to the United States will require an immigration visa. Processes involved includes filing your petition, processing your visa, final interview and medical examination.

Types of Visas

- Immigration for immediate family:

Foreign spouses can qualify for US citizenship under the immediate relative category. Others under this category includes:

- Parents and step-parents.

- Children and step-children below the age of 21.

- Spouses of US citizens who are dead.

To get this visa, you have to file a form 1-130 with the Citizenship and Immigration Services (USCIS).

- Family Based Visa for US Immigration

A citizen of the United States or a Lawful Permanent Resident are those who can file this claim. Eligible family members includes unmarried daughters or sons who are aged 21 or more than that of a citizen of the US, married sons/ daughters of a US citizen, brothers and sisters of a US citizen, and spouses and unmarried sons and daughters of an LPR.

- Academic Visa F1

Those who want to study in the United States need to acquire this visa. It covers a wide range of age, from primary to university level. Holders are allowed to enter the country 30 days before their course commences and to stay in the country 60 days after the completion of those courses. A student visa could serve as a pathway for a work permit if you gain experiences in an in-demand area of expertise. Non-academic visa M1 is available to those who are coming into the country for a non-academic course. Exchange students require an exchange visitor J1 Visa.

- Medical students

A B1 visa is required for a medical student that is registered in an overseas medical school to do an elective clerkship in the US.

www.ingramcontent.com/pod-product-compliance
Lightning Source LLC
Chambersburg PA
CBHW051224250726
48655CB00006B/2576